IN CONCERN:

for angels

IN CONCERN:

for Angels

BILL VARTNAW

ACKNOWLEDGEMENTS

Rainier Maria Rilke, I gratefully acknowledge as seed of this book. I had been reading *The Duino Elegies* & *The Sonnets to Orpheus* for several years when it suddenly occurred to me that I needed to know what an Angel was in my life.

A special thanks to Jane Roberts, Robert Butts, & Seth for their wonderful books & for setting such a loving & forthright example for exploring "the unofficial." I gratefully acknowledge their seeds also.

Thanks to all those mentioned in dedications above the poems in this book for inspiration &/or support. Especially Paula Gunn Allen who helped edit & organize this book & who supported me in this effort from her first contact with these poems. Thanks also to David Bromige, who helped me look at these poems from another perspective.

Thanks to Carol Lee Sanchez for helping me clarify my dream as book as well as for all her work, her support, & her friendship.

Thanks to Tim Jacobs, Jim Scott, & Tom Sharp for their work, their support, & their friendship.

Thanks to Gary Gach for his work & knowledge beyond the call of duty.

Thanks to George & Gladys Nitzberg for their support long before this book was even dreamed of.

Thanks to all those in my life I have failed to mention because they are not directly related to the publication of this book. I couldn't have done it just this way without you.

Cover design: Carol Lee Sanchez
Angel Sculpture: James A. Scott
Design & type: Gary G. Gach
Photography: Thomas Allen

ISBN 0-931552-05-2

To Grace Mendoza,
Somehow, Dear Cello,
This one's for you

Table of Contents
(By first line; titles, if any, appear in brackets after the poems)

Tree.   Stands.   Out.
Conversant with the mind
of light.   & its shifting interference—
in motion, winding:
like a splash.   Firmly rooted?
So it seems . . .
Tree, a master of disguises
spins dervishlike.   In synch
with times, familiar—
& throughout simultaneous existence,
to provide consistency.   The ground
is not so solid & is no anchor.
We have always dug our treasure
inside-out.   Tree is no exception.

In time-lapse, the shot from the satellite shows
the shape changing & approaching our shore.
"Voices," says the weatherman, using
his pointer, "carried by the Alaskan current
hit a high pressure system here . . .
What precipitates is a swirl,
        a heavenly chorus,
breaking off after this bend
                        into solos like jazz
& counterpointing the blue whales at 20 fathoms.
These are not seagulls with acne . . ."

[PORTENT]

I

*for Edwin Markham
& W. H. Auden*

The theory of evolution curls in a red tide
over Auschwitz, over & over.   Fish belly up,
slap against the shore, awaiting the wizard
to turn them into possum.   A step up the ladder
& another chance to draw from Community Chest.

How no one dared believe it.   Yet for others
so logical.   So methodical.   One might say,
"So business as usual."   The seeds we planted
at Sand Creek, at Wounded Knee, Evanston,
over & over.   How salvation would come in

completion.   Who calls these rocks inanimate?
This Earthy dirt from which spring begonias in
late summer?   How the past takes form, grows with us;
changes, no longer physical; yet neither are we,
the living present, that small 'trapped' sum.

We must speak of it often.   How the Earth spins
as it circles the sun.   I have seen the dead
buried.   They will not be forgotten.   No.   Never.
After each & every memorial & museum &
renovated relic crumbles into dust, the dead will

continue to flow through us, blood cell & tissue,
the deeds we have done.   The company that comes for dinner
each night will again tell us the great expense
of dredging up dinosaurs, how necessary
they are for bumper to bumper angst & whiplash

fortunes.   It's a fact.   My life   *is* easier
than John the Baptist's.   But there (& here) in exclusion
the complications begin.   I will never believe it.
No.   That if the theory is true, at one time &
one place, all has come to this & moves on . . .

[THE FOLDED LIE, THE TRUTH UNFOLDS]

The opening.   As if someone slit the surface
of an overripe Earth & the juice just rose up
through the rock to reveal itself.   Eel River, Fortuna.

You are here with friends.   One who knows
the area.   One who carries a field guide
with colored pictures of birds.
                              You sit on the bank,
on boulders extending from the tangle of branches
you squeezed through to get here.   A long left
(toward town) & a longer right slighted by the sun's glare.
Over there, across the way the river recedes
from the row of trees leaving a layered beach
complete with skipping stones.
                              In winter
when the water is high & a darker shade of green,
those trees are tested.   You think of the January failures
that contribute to this June panorama . . .

Suddenly, a bird bursts from the bushes cutting
the air with uneven geometry, flurry & dash,
dart.   "Definitely a swallow," your friend says
leafing quickly through the book.   "Here, this one—
a barn swallow, the rust-colored breast . . ."
This amazes you, not for the naming but what is not:
trees, bushes, birds you can hear, boulders & rocks . . .
The vision extends into the shadows of the shapes
you feel.   Coming from within.   Something deeper
than the sense of it (or any pronoun).   Like calm.
An immediate knowing.   That feeling, Angels.
The synchronicity extends through out. . .

Molecule.   Subatomic particle.   The long loping phrase
of a great blue heron heading west . . . To know each
& every name & to speak them in a moment.   The moment:
unnamed, unknown.   & still we try & often we extend

what we know.   Always we go beyond this—
into the realm of Angels.   Their siren song the silence
presents to us.
                    Circles in the river.
What a mouthful this swallow is.   How it dips,
dives its beak into the water.   The drops slip &
slam against the surface, reuniting the river in our eye
to our hearbeats & our souls . . . How we are carried
by this current to bend, to swell, to rush & to loose
these selves into that ocean that curls in upon itself
to greet us.   The Angels' song permeates all
from that timeless within.   Moving in & out of focus
in & out of form.   Like those drops my swallow spills.

I know nothing but this feeling.   To have it broken
like that row of trees.   A whole in the middle
where mountains miles away rise, stunning
in their great green coats.   How it all changes . . .
The higher flying heron replaced by the kingfisher
looking for a meal.   The river's the constant
& the river isn't, as sun sparkles from the bobbing
current crests.   The process of choice.
I wonder what my eye sees in its own completeness.
This feeling remains, joyous in its own . . .

for Jim Krusoe

In the principal's office—
they got a guillotine that cuts off your tongue
if you talk too much without raising your hand.

I play with army men in the sandbox
& dig tunnels to China trying to escape.

Behind the incinerator next to the tetherball court—
they burn little boys with grass stained britches
who won't quit giggling during the air raid drill.

In the nurse's office—
they give electric shock treatment to little girls with glasses
who aren't brains & scribble a lot in their textbooks.

I climb trees & make forts
& attack the world with a rubber band & bobbie pins.

Inside one of the janitor's closets—
they got a gas chamber they lock you in
if they catch you throwing a spit wad at the clock.

I lay on my towel after "milktime" & dream of this day,
I can blow up the world.

[R U M O R S]

Your beauty is not enough.   Not like it used to be.
When I start looking for Angels,
soon they're all over.   I feel—the Unutterable—
& say : why didn't I see them before.

Beauty has become too vague.   A talent,
a tool, a joy & "only the beginning
of a terror" says the poet in translation.
Our work is all translation.   We are beholden.

In the beginning I'd run in front of oncoming traffic
simply to pick up a loosed & flying form.   "This is
for me !   I have given it value."   I'd say to myself
& feel touched.   Now, looking into a sky of eyes,

the past unrequited—more beautiful than before—
the young one returns—that tremor—& with him,
the memory : that terrible pelting of Angels !
Ah yes, Dear Ones, my needs, too, have changed.

. . . Wings wow me
beyond distinctions.   Hummingbirds hovering
in English.   The medium is the messenger.
We must see a feeling world.   I sometimes stroll—
in Atmospheres—spaces where material objects fade
like a car passing on a country road.   Lost
in thoughts, you enter a room
where everyone is speaking a language foreign to you.

You hear several voices at once, music.
There is more.   Too much.   The room has windows.
Landscapes with trees.   Leaves falling.   You are
standing still.   The room is.   The voices . . .
& snow starts gathering into drifts.
                    "Stop!"
& out of the corner of your eye, there's an Angel
laughing.   You turn & it escapes that kind of vision.

You face the silence, the eyes turned toward you.
How silly this all must look.   You want to create
the illusion of "no big thing" & so the idea occurs:
it was just the play of light & shadow . . .
                    No.   You named what you saw.
"That's better," you say. "Does anyone speak English?"
The room changes color.   The windows disappear
& now there are paintings in ornate gilt frames.

A hummingbird & a hollyhock.   You're reminded—
a Titian: a painting with an Angel & the Virgin.
                    . . . a Renaissance Angel.
"Well," you say, "I'll soon put a stop to that!"

World War I in an American Legion cap,
short stiff steps behind a four-legged cane
through tenderloin trenches
        & into the R & R of low cost housing . . .
paid monthly by the social security
        of 9.2 howitzer memories & muggings
& the gab of other old scars & wrinkles,
reinforcing a world-view: hell is growing
old in American cities.

We were great then;
broke isolation for the ideal & volunteered
        to run like crazy
through the shrapnel & charcoal whore
        we made of the old world
spitting bullets & the sperm of tough talk
bottled in melting pot frustration
& the stench of ghetto walk-ups.

We were all whores then;
but whores with a dream
& that was better than being . . . peasants!

World War I shuffles the dirt between soul & concrete;
he must catch up with the pace he sets for himself
in this transvestite night of neon necromania
where "danger" jumps like a stairway junkie
        from the thresholds of shadow
dedicated to the unknown soldier & other prisoners of war.
He pushes on . . .
        to where the porno palace marquee radiates safety;
he waits at the red light with the laughter of a corner hooker
while steel horses strafe the intersection with obnoxious odors
& the flash of ear-splitting sirens.

We were heroes then, with a job to do.

All around, there is nothing but devotion to purpose:
The gray-skinned panhandlers wrapped in blankets & lice
      scrounging through trash cans for their lunch . . .
The holes in the ground . . .
The blood-stained mud below the scream of bullets . . .
The senseless bodies . . .
      & the bodies writhing with wounds
            & dismemberment . . .
The red & ruddy-faced drunk
      passed out & cursing on apartment house steps . . .
The screaming three-time loser, hands cuffed behind him,
      pushed head first into the powder blue
            police services car . . .
Crawl over these monuments of manhood.
Feel the rub of flesh & khaki & blood & Earth & horror & bone
& self-hatred . . .

Waiting . . .
waiting & waiting for nightfall, for help from the trenches . . .
Caught in the no man's land
between the button & the breaking point
in the search & destroy mindset of father knows best:
fact finding/fault finding/perfect binding
& the sweet perversity of how much can you take.

The vet in pointed cap & cement shoes
pushes his purple heart
through the shellshock of general headquarters,
      Home of the Brave,
till he again reaches relative safety in the hut two three
      of his room
where he can fall back on his bed,
look up at the ceiling
& think about the good old days.

[WIN & END ALL WARS]

There is a sense of Grace I wish
to achieve, to accompany
my every expression.   The culture of Angels.

Just ten years ago, my ambition was Sainthood.
I found it uplifting to say No,
to have little to do with this world around me.

Taking a taste, I would enjoy & then deny,
enjoying my sense of will.   Oh, Bliss!
How complacent you are.   This is not the way

of Angels.   Angels are sots.   They relish
in their formlessness.   No eyes, no mouth & still
they drink.   They see things differently, beyond

the continuums of a lifetime.   Wishing to be
their tongue, I must be their throat,
their stomachs & the balls of their feet as well.

They enlist my whole body & observe me
with the compassion you watch a child learning
to walk.   Of course, it's impossible!   All we can be—

is a rough distortion.   We've chosen our limitations
as we stretch ourselves into spaces of Earth
no less real than geography.   It is not a consolation—
this stretching nourishes us.   All of us.

Art & nature are imitations, not of each other, but of the same third thing—both images of the real, the spectral & vivid reality that employs all means. —Muriel Rukeyser, *The Life of Poetry*

Looking down from the precipice
to the open space . . .   It's sexual.
A chorus of Angels whisper in my ear,
others tug at my guts, urging strongly
toward freedom.   Toward death.
(They prefer to advertise the freedom.)
I do not understand my feelings.   Falling
as if I did
            jump—

This is no Bible story.   There is no devil here,
no Christ being tempted.   There is a quest
in questioning.   The Angels know
this freedom they present & ignore
the focus I have chosen.   I feel threatened
& summon Earth into my decisions—the gravity—
noted in the nature of events, an attraction
toward the core.   I center myself accordingly.
Earth upholds each step we make.   Collects it:
360 degrees.   An infinite supply of circles,
one moment . . .

My active senses make
me—a part & parcel of this vision.
This is my beauty.   This is my nature,
more elaborate than my words.
Pine sap, granite & blood.   I present it
gift-wrapped.   The power.   Echoed—
in this outer nature.   I am equal to it.   We are.
I am to you a messenger.   My words are
from the same source.   So many languages
converging in one room & moving out again
like the sea, leaving foam on the shore
of our cells.   Soaking in.

Looking back: the precipice, the Angels
singing.   I was not prepared to hear:

re-lease.   A new contract,
new language.   An agreement to set apart
a creator—
            from the physical (creations . . .
& to inhale them all together again,
as most intimate self moves
from intricate dust to the core
of what leaves the body behind.
A more discriminating consciousness.
I bring my beauty here:
to this meeting place of Angels,
where what seems is only the beginning.
& what is dissipates into the sweet intelligence
that knows
            no limits—

The choices we made to lose touch . . .

To become phantoms.   Another person.   I stood in a crowd
looking up.   The lead ball swung by the crane.   Boom!
There is a fascination.   How much the structure can take.
How the impact turns to rubble below.   Dust flies.
We are made of this.   Up from the foundation, the framework
often bends to unlikely degrees before collapsing.   Boom!
Each rivet registers each blow.   One by one, the crowd leaves
stunned by the building's strength.   The machine's power.
The waste.   The marked absence in the making.   In time,
the debris will be cleaned up & hauled away.   To new purposes
or simply junked.   The clean space will hardly seem natural.

> I think of Kneeland's quiet intensity.   Driving
> down the middle.   The foul.
> The anger.   Drawing us closer
> into the bounds of group & self-consciousness.
> Thompson's laughter
> after a set-shot: *swish!*
> It was psychic
> how some plays were so pretty,
> pick & roll:
> a pass the moment I broke to the basket.
> We sense each other's moves,
> keep moving: the magic! We grow,
> let each other know immediately.
> There is an agreement between us:
> as one gets better, we all improve
> or 'the game' loses . . . interest
> Everhart became a threat from the corner.
> Hearney banks the ball off the backboard.
> Ankles & elbows reach for the rebound:
> "Take it back!"

Our memory changes things.   Makes them current.   Within

the structure of present opinion & belief.   Buildings
that now stand like skeletons (or holes in the ground) will become
meaty with walls & plumbing.   In our excitement,
we may not consider that what is gone grows on without us.
We may not hear the hoary-haired individual say, "Oh sure,
I know where that is, you mean where the old pyramid building
used to be."   Boom!   We are carriers of each other's identity.
At each moment, we choose who we are & who agrees.

[CONTACT SPORT]

Pow-wow.   A convergence.   I bring the Angels here.
They were here all the time, though I didn't know—
didn't recognize them as such—wanting something
everyone could see, like fry bread & beans.

People, nations & ways dancing to the drum.
A center.   It is not mine, not here, not in this life.
I cannot dance.   It would not be right.   & so
I watch.   Look in.   Friends dance, claiming a who

they are.   Each of us reaching in our own way, out
& in, to the center we create continually
from what we know of being & what we don't . . .
I created the Angels to center myself.   Like Earth,

on one level.   An event growing out of other events
not necessarily occurring in time.   Or being
the effect of any visible cause.   The silence
between drumbeats.   The movement beyond the steps.

What I was becomes a symbol.   & I am changing
flesh, moving away from child's sorrow, wanting
to lighten my heart with love, to trust the rainbow
I have created.   Tearing open the spaces, I dance

in-conspicuously.   Apart.   & a part of the silence,
the movement, the dance that continues . . .

for Tom Sharp

Once there was a time when it was necessary
to remove our selves from nature.   Once.
To distinguish, to see within
these selves is the objective.   It's second nature

now.   This chain-of-being buried
& nearly forgotten.   Paved over in sediment
like walled in cities, lessons in childhood,
other experiences qualified or in need of

the missing link.   "Man is held highest on Earth
& below the Angels."   The intention:
toward God.   Then later, toward a controlled state—
technology.   The competition is fierce

& it is not.   An Angel (many?) who inhabits
the rock suggests you skip its flat surface
on the river.   Interfacing the world of eyes,
you pick it up: sentient self awareness

beyond the organs of particularity.   Yes, you are
the rock & each plant & animal whose dust
compresses here.   A moment of your time.
It is easiest to relate to the air.   You fill of it.

& who & what it has been wears your blood
like a coat—becoming it, becoming warm.
You begin to see the choices, how desire determines
the who of you.   The chain dissolves into Angels.

You skip the rock across the river, letting go.
We have become both worlds now.

II

Inside the office, hanging plants swing
planet rhythms.   Typing stops.   Bug-eyed
secretary searches the room for agreement
& instant awe.   "Is it?"   The tree in the corner
rustles its leaves, "Sha sha."   Paper stillness.
I am in this room, stories above the street

cement, in a building on a rumbling ground
with an idea: All this could tumble!
"What is it I want to do?"   I am safe.
The tremor has stopped for now.   We're left

holding a snake by its rattles.   "Have faith,
my boy, have faith."   The six o'clock news will
offer unbelievers a reading from the Richter scale
& photos from The Big One.   (Science,
a wonderful sedative.)   & like the good old days,
we wait . . .

II

No victims, we.   This ground.   Our stand
on life.   & detente.   These plates below us.
The shifting.   A "5" this time.   Our failure
to predict the next one, then the next . . .
Lessons all over the place, but no verbs.
A poet in an office building.   In the routine:
Eight.   Nine.   Ten: break.   Eleven.   Twelve-
thirty: lunch.   A house of mirrors.   Infinite
regression.   The space between, light years!

III

Most is measured, not understood.   Chiselled.
I have wished to speak of contribution & fallen
short.   "Not there."   I'd say, "But not here either.
Yet."   The fault line.   Do I want to break off
the part that holds me back & throw it in the ocean?

& sink it.   What good is it?   I want to know that more.
The now in know.   In awe, we remember the epicenters
of time.   The moment.   & how quickly it can change

momentum.   The reverberations out.   Precognized within
the animal.   Taken by technology & distributed
via the air waves.   For what stands under me is me
in a bigger world that grows through us like breathing.

[E A R T H Q U A K E C O U N T R Y]

There!   Angels.   Where the river runs
into the ocean.   A crystal
conceived by you in the provinces of Paris
forms a covalence with the salt,
the Pacific.   This long moment rises . . .

A flat choppy surface.   & above, the flap & drag.
pelicans!   & their long neck, long beak
belly flops behind the curling manufacture
of white water.   (Here, it is said,
we washed up upon the shore . . .

At best, this is a metaphor
to say we came from the nothingness
that is everywhere alluded to.)   This meeting
of mediums.   Of land & sea, that air provides.
Of life & death, that serve this conscious moment.

The word.   Yes!   Angels gather here, carried
by the current to the moon's easy tide.
O spontaneous sun-drenched phrases!
Will you believe it when I tell you
this ocean is both future & past?   & the clouds

more than punctuation that ciphens meaning
for a rain.   Just beyond this reach
& its undertow, your adept eyes scan the beach
for that desired feeling, "Exactly right!
Yes, this Angel fits me well . . ."

[CIPHERS, SIPHONS]

for John Goodman

Identify any commonly understood act
of suspicious circumstances

Shadows arise each morning.   We wake
without much effort to find *"a substantive manifestation*
of a yet unexplained phenomena."   We say:
This is my world.   The bush, a shifting shape,
"Interplay with the wind."   I say it's different,
even its roots . . .   Things can move so quickly,
we choose not to speak, to slow it down
to a size—something separate, living
its own life like stories in the newspaper.
"Too many people have experienced too much
in completely unrelated incidents."   Beyond the what
as focus.   Or as claim.

It is easier with love.   We can pick & choose.
Swap molecules, saliva, words.   Spin the web
of Angels.   I think of Grace who is in Berkeley &
she is with me.   *The feeling of independence*
& self-confidence, the feeling of creativity
have dignfied, have honored & have encouraged
lives of high spirits . . . My contract as poet says nothing
about keeping up with page 1.   Somebody will.
I choose the news from my own sources.   I know
what's going on.   Not in so many words, but enough.

Identity may become part of a large scale data bank.
The man who sits behind the bus driver all rummy
& kind.   Always a nice word for everybody
& his dog.   The same nice word.   I do not want to save
the world.   To love it—if I can do that . . . yes
We do not live in an authoritarian system
where you can expect people to obey . . .
What can he be thinking?   Not me!   I say, knowing
that's not completely true.   He's a part of me—
a shadow shifting.   The winds of my psyche . . .
I change that quickly.   I don't know why
I want you to know that, but I do.
I change that quickly.

Italicized fragments taken from the San Francisco Chronicle

Half of me is third generation.

"& I shall tell you more.   There is no birth in mortal things & no
end in ruinous death.   There is only mingling & interchange of
parts, & it is this that we call 'nature.'"   (Empedocles)

This country is founded on Protestant principles.
He kept singing "We Shall Overcome"
as he marched through concrete streets &
heard his words echo off the walls
of government & the dead
bodies that lie within the lines
the electron gun fired upon the picture tube
into his brain
                    until he was hoarse & crying.
Little mingling occurred.
He was at war with a world at war
& no less explosive.
Thinking back, it was the catholicity of the experience
I abhor.

Though half of me is third generation,
all of me was born here & continues to be.

"Into the same river, I step & do not step."   (Heraclitus)

Authorities were immediately defensive
"There is no danger."   Instruments read, reflected:
something beyond the senses is happening here
that cannot be explained
mathematically.   The pope is Polish.
In the home for unwanted ideas, a leader,
whose time has come, gets up on an orange crate
& beckons others:
                    "Reclaim yourself."
At once, gangs of ideas roam the night streets looking
for love & a place to hang out.   Emotion literally squeals to be
                    [seen, as it races up & down narrow avenues
boxed in metal.   Almost nostalgically,
the unwanted become feared;

their exuberance incomprehensible to a solid-state system.
Not even the suggestion of an Excedrin headache seems to
                              [calm these urges into respectability.
A tornado in Texas, an earthquake in San Francisco,
these are to be expected at times like this.
Foundations are moving!

"I am the most widely travelled man of all my contemporaries,
& have pursued inquiries in the most distant places; I have
visited more countries and climes than anyone else, & have
listened to the teachings of more learned men. No one has
surpassed me in the drawing of lines accompanied by dem-
onstrations, not even the rope-knotters of Egypt, with whom I
passed five years on foreign soil . . . I came to Athens & no one
knew me."   (Democritus)

                              [GREEK TO ME]

Stretching out.   Images blur . . .
On the rope swing at the lake.   Acceleration
& the old agreements don't hold
true.   I'm hesitant.

I was hesitant before.   Dropping slow-
motion into a flood of feeling.
Faces on the street.
Intense attraction.   Let go—

Falling in . . .
No, I need a new language.
What I feel isn't literal,
it's energy.   We're moving

off in our own directions . . .
Never mind.
I feel closer somehow
to everyone

concerned.   I love them
not because they agree.
We've grown through that & each other,
following

the example of Angels.
The scene is similar:
a few hours
before the last time. . .

Only now there is no taunting,
no looking inside
for proof—just off the rock
                        & go . . .

I-5, avenue of Volcanoes.   The processes
of this movement are unknown to me.   Desire,
the initial energy.   Invisible as dreams.   Indivisible
with that mountain that I seek here.   An aspect of

Earth's power that feels so different from the quake
country I'm used to.   A "there" you can stare at
with awe.   The harmony of shape & color
in time.   How substantial the trees

like a deep groaning sigh below that seemly (or seeming) solid-
ity.   The disciplined geometry
of manmade structures.   "The eye is not enough,
it is necessary to reflect."   The world of Angels.

We attempt to count in dollars: trees
snapped & up-rooted, dragged in molt & sludge
down to the river bloated with life's blood
of these surroundings.   A front page spread.

Land & weather tied visibly to a concept.   Ash all over.
Road signs point the direction.   The news paints
my experience of what these turn-offs could present.
New growth emerges from this land laid bare.

Rainier.   Hood.   Shasta.   Each alone, silent . . .
austere.   Labeled by their past & therefore potential.
Asleep within the sophistication of language.
& dreaming the dreams of mountain, cell & Earth.

The processes of this movement are unknown to me
& yet I do move quite smoothly through the land
of Angels.   Pre-sense.   Impulsive & solid as the radio
signal that tells me Helens has the hiccups again.

We are not helpless but meant to know this power
that aligns us & how it makes us feel   more
conscious of our human connection—the interaction of
powered planes, a dynamic sense of depth & direct contact.

Angels recognize no difference.
I saw neither with my two eyes
nor my third . . .

       I

Lying in my bed, the dark.
Light came through from the living room.
A baseball bat under my pillow.
I watched my grandmother waste away.
She was brave for me, I never knew
her pain . . .
           A presence.   I could feel it
& feeling it, I leaned & it was solid.
& yet I knew if I did not believe,
this feeling would give way —
the laws we've agreed upon.   I wondered:
Is this my grandmother?
Not knowing, I felt reassured
& leaned into dreams . . .

       II

Quick.   Expected.   The heart.
I crouched over his life.   He entered
& I shared: a father comforting his daughters.
I did not doubt — though she was older
& in that calm, he left . . .

Nothing would be the same.   It never is.
All we know, these moments.
The Angel's face changes always & always
there's an angle you've never caught before.
To loose.   To rattle.   To re-mind you.

In the living room of my innocence,
I watched them march to DC
on TV—the day he told the world
his dream.   & I entered.   & I was ashamed . . .
How small I was . . . I cried
for the wrong reasons.

Entering a new world.   Angels remind us
"This is not the old world."
Something moves within me like wind
blowing, showing off its power,
changing shapes like a dream.

I was protected for the best of reasons.
Who were they who told me "Don't
trust what you feel, learn to see things
our way"?   Why did I believe them?
Under the circumstances, forgiveness is easy.
Relax.   Enter & re-lease.

The flesh is weak
        & trembles with passion.
        2 heads : 10 toes :
Flow of blood igniting a tingle of nerve ends.
            a triangle sharp resonance ;
                clear & quivering.
I note the fear :
hair on end / cool air around body radiating rhythms
& heat.

This is mine.   This is me.
This is who I have to give you,
tumescent with the spark of foreplay
        the touch
        the brush of fingertips.
I reflect in the deep rich color of your eyes . . .

I note the fear ; its relation —
        this pull toward you, its strength
        acceleration.
                        I am not so solid : you are
within me, the molecules of my composition take
a path of least resistance
            further into myself, drawn to
            this place where I meet you
— not in my own image, but a timeless space.
& yes, I know we are always spinning & of the Earth
        & undivided in process of breath's embrace.
& yet, what frightens me : this multiplicity.
You are woman & within me, & the others of yourself.
Who am I ?

The flesh is weak
        & wants to make moments hard as bone,
        tender as a baby's cry.
Flood of feeling

blood of my father's only child / a name to pass on
I tremble . . .
I have these words :
    propelled by my lungs
    pushed out into the air, sustaining
        this material claim to being.
They are my words,
    weighted sounds
    fall as stones to the ground I walk on, say :
Yes, in all of this & am I alone, too,
                                & changing ?

I tremble . . .
& beyond my understanding, my cells echo
    in their completeness
to loosen the rigidity of this 'individual' misconception
    & give strength
to remember the many countenances
    I have chosen
    to clothe my present & call 'world,'
this evernew 'me' we are creating, & 'you'.
This is a primal value of nature :
    the nourishing blood sustains
    & returns to the heart for nurture.

The flesh is weak
so our greater being may be known.
I am growing, growing always,
having grown.

[T H E   R e U n i o n]

For if there are Angels, & there are,
there are Guardian Angels.   They held me together
when my American dream died & I was
forced to look at myself as an entity

older than my lifetime.   I chose to be—
born white & male when that dominance was dying
to a bigger world.   & that small town
upbringing was/is part of me—pseudo-superiority—

as I wield myself into more open spaces . . . Now,
the quick planet shimmers & I see we live (bleed)
through each other—like the personalities of Sybil—
cultivating images to integrate or discard . . .

Each of us—bigger than life—the world made
more obvious than metaphors from the silver screen,
the magazines from Los Angeles.   Angels breathe
dimension into all the slick flat surfaces we seek.

From outside of time, they appear in future residence
& in my past like footprints through a desert.   Here, always
the oasis—the Guardian refreshment—the aim
re-membered through its challenges.   The shifting contours.

The wind of consensus.   A burning sun.   Refracted.
The appropriate facts ample like sand.   A blindman stands
at each turn holding a beggar's cup.   Do not lose sight . . .
The Angels will see us through.

for James A. Scott

How does a tree grow?   The men pay
no attention, play bocce ball or whatever
they call it in Arles.   Clack.   The game must be
intense.   Whitehat hunches over, elbows on knees.
His wood chair is solid.   Sycamore sap
jams the trunk & branches with daily dramas.

Whitehat is not a bowler.   I am not
fluent in French.   I do not know the objective
of this game.   The balls are all in broad daylight.
The men talk loudly, in congratulatory tones.
The wind blows to the horizon where haze breaks
into blue.   None of this helps me remember . . .

Some force from inside must push out . . .
The tree thickens.   I was in Italy 11 years ago.
On a beach in a town south of Naples.   The name
started with an "S," I think.   Men bowled & baited,
I watched & was invited to play.   Cells duplicate
themselves.   One becomes two becomes 4.

We learn the rules we teach the rules keep
changing.   The tree digs into earth, becomes.   Stays.
Leaves.   The wind heaves.   Neither the foliage
nor the fabric of their clothes can hold it.
Blackslacks bends at the waist to urge his ball on.
Clack.   Palermo.   Was that it?   Palermo?

Each season is seen here.   Pruned & knobby,
these plane trees glow with memory from the ground
up.   Pressure greater than gravity.   On his last try
Yellowshirt hit the smaller ball away from the others.
The game may last forever.   Slow, or seemingly so,
each moment has always contained the next . . .

[T H E   B O W L E R S]

In the dark, smoke & Angels filter through
a cone illuminated above our heads.   A circle
develops into a rectangle.   I sat watching.
They are stuck in a room.   The door is open.

It's funny—the butler doesn't do a thing but serve.
& still, one of them dies.   Surreal.   Perhaps
I exaggerate.   This is a time of religion.
The angels that speak to them are made in plaster

molds.   I watch what I thought was
crumble.   Piles of dust.   & the pieces won't fit
together the way I thought they should.
That doesn't seem to matter.   This matters—

& how these frames projected almost a decade ago
connect.   Time reels from every speck of space
driven by the moments between thought.   Only now
do I realize   I have walked through that door.

Familiar, everchanging . . .
A commitment.   A regulation.
Being with friends, I watch them:
the speaking & the listening.   Tossing worlds around . . .
What is familiar?   I see Angels crowd in, behind
each movement.   At each moment
a singular Angel breaks through the balance.
Your hive of responses.   The swarm—
possibilities converted into an identity.   Purposeful,
a making: thick liquid in a powercell.
Your eyes ignite—the Charge—& the Angel enters
through the periscope I project toward our meeting
& wraps us as a mother would button her child's coat
in winter.   We become her construction &
our gracious hostess invites others to her stead.
Soon, the too of us buzz, thick with Angels . . .

Do you remember a first Angel?   Perhaps
you had been waiting, wanting.
You could feel your own Angels pacing, scheming:
a new way to communicate.   Clear to you,
it is what you yearned for.
Every Angel knew—for they move outside of time.
It happens so quickly.   You create the event.
The Angel came.   A "realization."
It was not how you imagined it to be.   The finding.
More, always more was involved.
& you said philosophically, "Well, that's the way it is."
This, the Angel's signature—a disappointment, a delight—
Your friend, always
a little more than you wanted . . .

& what of yourself?
Familiar, everchanging . . .
What manifests?   & from where?
"Something, somewhere."   You answer.
Will it last forever?   Or is it like an Angel —
a life of its own.   & so close,
an Angel can blind us like a mirror.
We may even be ignorant we hold on.   & if we do . . .
we notice rather the anxious moments,
or their characteristic compulsions
as the Angel works itself free.   Then it comes —
as a thought or a stranger on the street,
a reminder: *wu-wei*.   The rule applies to both sides.
In the middle, I
& the familiar: something, somewhere.

Wu-wei: "not doing," the meaning of which is not "doing nothing" but "not forcing."
—Joseph Campbell, *Myths To Live By*

III

Entering toes first,
but mistakenly spread-eagle,
the baptism was mildly abrupt
& cool
as afterimages of craggy landscapes
accompanied my immersion
& its associative bubble massage.
Surfacing
I'm a new man—
a bit angrier for my lack of form . . .

for David Bromige

The stream of water
perfect & continuous
to the eye & hand.

The strobe—
frozen motion
focus : globules

White water / stilled / by a jet to L.A.

I offer Angels—
consciousness connecting
each focus perfect to the next . . .

True for water as for rock,
for crumpled car fender
& its "before"

as for pear, its devourer
whether (man or beast) or bug
or both.

Like jet lag.   The pull from an unknown.
The connection, abstracted & otherwise
taken for granted, is within-geography.
The gravity of this situation is not grave.

& gray matter, my blue skies, is the point
of departure.   I am air born.
These hills I dwell upon are the wavelengths
of my soul.   I do not strive for mountain tops

but find elevation in speaking from my heart.
My words are layered & ringed.   Redwood trees
rooted to the Earth but from another source.
My body quakes like a wind-loosed branch

each time I say good-bye.   An Angel falls.

for Tom Sharp

The voice inside interrupts the traffic
on the street, "You gotta make time.
Make time." Others have their answers
& are eager to give advice & it sounds
good, within the context they present.
It could be a sign or a choice
not taken. One pigeon
in that flock that flutters overhead
looking for a handout. Seldom
do we distinguish one from the other.
"It's just a pigeon." Something that flies
in & out of our lives. Even less
do we give names to these free ones. But O!
to see a big bird in the country . . .
That makes us feel special. & why not?

There's an attraction you never admitted
before. You want to try for incorporation.
You meet with resistance—a who you are
that's not like them. So involved,
you can break it down to a series of symptoms.
Past mirrors. Then it occurs to you: a rumor.
"You know what I just heard? See all this
pigeon shit. It's not what it seems.
They're communicating with super-intelligence
out in space with very intricate sensors
that scan Earth. They use an accumulative language
beyond our comprehension. Each new dropping
creates a new conceptual mode of understanding
& simultaneously adds to a world-wide message unit
that takes into account the spinning Earth's relation
to the sensor. These pigeons are very precise
about what they say & where they say it . . .
Look at that windshield. Amazing, isn't it?"

Who'd believe it?   Here you are in the park
looking at the ruffled neck feathers
of that pigeon.   You wonder what he sees
in her.   Spinning, chasing her like that . . .
Quite a display of determination.   Yesterday
on the same ledge with the same dance, the same partner.
She flew away.   He followed.   You wonder
where he finds the time.   The old man with bread crumbs;
you worry, he's usually quite punctual.
There's such a temptation to sell yourself cheap,
to just get the information out to whoever wants it.
You must re-member you are one of them.   A piece
in the puzzle you are so fond of.   It is the pieces
that must be emphasized, not how they fit together.
"Ah, here's the old man!"   In their excitement,
pigeons beat the air with ungrounded assertions.
"My God," you think.   "Look at the spaces between!"

[PIGEON POEM]

So, what have we here?

Wings?   I hear voices, feel urges.
Angels live outside this dance,
like telepathy.   I suspect my importance.

A wristwatch of Angels, this feeling between us.
The phone rings.   Intricate circuitry.   Relays.
A black deer circumscribed over a white fish.
The receiver: I am a completed moment,

Angel.   A reflexive act.
Down an otherwise empty street, an army
more populous than the Earth—We turn away

Hello?   Who is this?

Thanks to : Linda Louis
Carol Lee Sanchez
Paula Gunn Allen
Judy Grahn

The pain, I said, I don't want the pain.
I don't want to cause it, to bear it
through the silence of years,
to anything . . . . Just leave me alone
to do what I do.   What can I say
to ease your harried heart ?

Your thoughts in my mind.
You once told someone,
"My strings touch the stars."
& now, here you are, cold,
getting colder ; the delicate instrument
you held so proudly —
"a traitor in yours arms. "
Death is in the air.
You take big breaths.

You felt you could do anything.
Your mother, father told the neighbors :
"My child has talent.   A musician
with gifts that'll add beauty
to this world of ours. "   The neighbors.
Aren't they the ones throwing rocks
& spitting in your direction ?

Dead to this time, you are in my past
& more real than many
a fleshy passerby.   I am in the future,
unknown.   We meet, timeless,

48

in a space travelled by inner senses
& imagination, something akin
to "only a feeling" & a bad bad dream.
I am not "you" nor are you "me"
nor will you be.   Yet I will not deny
a consciousness we share, a well of being
we drink from, a bubbly we both enjoy, . . .

So how can I ease your pain?
by giving in to it?   To suffer for you?
To rage again & feel powerless
as I ask: How can anyone do this
to another?   & again judge
bind myself to the acts of man only
& ignore this inner world,
this greater dependence that connects us,
living & dead . . .

Your violin reaches me through time.
Not as sound, but a feeling—
a coughing up, a swallow going down
the wrong pipe.   A reflex,
spontaneity intent on survival,
fulfillment.

How I have leaned on you in this life—
to create the model: a pain worth living for,
something to endure, to share with men.
I marvel at your abilities & strength;
but to play for the mercy of murderers . . .
Tell me, does this make you right?

It's a tree that grows cheese in plastic . . .
You say, "My faith in man grows sour."

You have entered into a world of people
who agree with you—
for their own reasons, in their own ways.
"Murderers" you say,
but not as to draw attention to yourself.
That's easy to accept.
The scary thing is they're more powerful
& so are you . . .

Writing this, my life changes—
I watch the connections as symbols
in a dream.   I understand the why of how
I people this moment.   & you're included.
Just now, the silhouette of your longish face.

I thank you—that tough-mindedness
that sometimes dreadful earnestness
you bequeathed me.   I've made it mine.
It serves me, perhaps saves me at times,
but I'm tired: holding the world
at arms' length, fearing an image—
something you think we deserve:
life's been too good to us . . .

Follow an endless ray of sun endlessly radiating.
Yes you are part of me, you're part of many;
I am.   I reject often: truths you gave your life for.
The burden of guilt passes into regret
I can share, a small scar I can live with
without loss of movement
or feeling.

[T o   a   P a s t   S e l f]

I enter through the gate
already opened . . .
                        Piles of lumber
weathering & the rusty frame of a car
or two . . .
            I expect a presence

but instead a snake,
instead a gosling, a pupping sniffing
my shoes, raccoon cub . . .
                        A yard full—
Animals, newly born & not necessarily tame
but indigenous.   At peace.
        Only when I see the wildcat
sitting on the feedhouse steps

                        do I realize
what he has become,
                    had been all the time . . .
        & that these animals begin here
          & grow into themselves

                        [T W O W E E K S L A T E R] ..

Whatever had drawn us, drew us.
The familiar basket catch, the punctual push off
the hamstrings, the strike to the plate . . .
Moments—the coordination.   Hero, you return.
This concrete shell.   & I am here—
what I saw, what I heard, what I know you did.

My childhood.   The tear on my cheek.   I dare
not move—the hot dog vendor will intrude
my intimate joy.   "Old timer," the gifts
that made you famous have waned & still I cheer—
you who I knew mostly through declarative fragments
from the radio, statistics in the sporting green.

I made worlds from your talents.   You swing
& I hear 40,000 fans groan ecstatic at the possibilities
one moment could present.   Yes.   The season ended.
& I wandered off building up new heroes to tear down,
to leave behind in a gesture of growth.   A striving
in opposition to the embrace of Angels,

their inter-connectedness.   This patchwork
that defies time.   A continuous moment.   Broken
by years & unrelated Angels.   Hero, diamond clarity
returns in context, with new appreciations
that vivify all my experience.   I remain unbroken:
a world series of continuing moment . . .

for Grace Mendoza

The essential ingredient
for turning any – into the most
elegant . . . The offer
that denies the present.   The gift   we already have
to give.   *To take advantage*
of this unique opportunity, simply
tell us . . . I have been saving these (words)
unwittingly.   My world —
I do not control it or want to.   I'm not at war.
I live here with billions of others
under a jackhammer rain, images of
the goodlife   *So if you're the kind who takes*
pride   in both the quality &   the news.
A promise   it'll all be paved over
soon.   *Smooth & fresh all the way* . . .

The scars & wondering how   do I bring
myself   new to you.   Myself
in the mirror, talents & experience
thumbtacked to the wall in back of me.
& those probabilities
looming, blooming in the shadows & depths,
stirred by the overhead fan.   World,
she is t(here) for me.   A partner & a friend,
a lover.   I love her.   She will not save me.
I do not need her to.
                    I choose this
parentage of pain & to let go —
Not a retreat to innocence,
the ambiguity becomes part of my nature as you do.
Developed with space   age technology
that goes into e v e r y t h i n g   I do — all of it,
what & who.   It's not simple.   You're here
for yourself, for me.   As I am . . . we
Research has shown Love is infinite
& not a scarce commodity.   You are   like & unlike me.
& more than I dreamed or remember dreaming.

But like a lot of people, I'm aware of
The in-group extortion.   The failure of any religion
spread through the sociology of its borders.
Your uniqueness appeals to me.   *It stands*
to reason, really.   A radiance:
Beauty.   Talent.   Intelligence.
I love you now knowing change is inevitable.
Wishing strength, I write
in weakness.   The teacher.   The influential elder.
The more you understand, the more likely
A phase of the moon.   Woman, you are just
as much Sun as I am.   & Moon.   & Earth.
May we grow together.   May our orbits be open.
& our radiance bring understanding to the darkness
ahead . . .

I've created you in my life.   Thoughts,
actions that called you in.   *Pictures that come*
to life — in minutes — right before your
Desire & doubt (though not about you).
You created me too.   *A breed apart.*
I don't know who you see completely.   I am.   &
I am an amalgam of each projection.   An object
in every person's life who claims to know me.
The next best thing to being there.   Suddenly,
here & pulling.   Our meeting — described
in deeper terms: something, somewhere.
Doing what we do best.   A yesterday with no clues . . .
You seemed much older.
Now, a long time ago.   (So many changes.)
Love, the whole is timeless.
Now is all.   The ideal breaks the moment.
Soft lips, that spot on my neck you found—

sends goose pimples to my ankles.   I've stepped
away from this writing several times
to gather inspiration . . .

& it's just the beginning, like memory.   A way of
coming to.   We are not doomed
to repeat it.   To live only to die
within the safety of this coincidence of love.
Here, clearly, would be something of permanence
in a changing & uncertain   I
do not fear it.   Myself.   The moment.   The poem changes, the Poem
remains.   The Angels have taught me to walk.
To believe in.   & then, return.
Memory tells of other moments & no logic
but myself.   I had to laugh.
& though, *We have the figures to prove it*
or otherwise.   I find I grow in leaps & bounds
& carry you with me wherever . . .

*I*nclusion.   Take something easy.   A textbook
says the Sun is 93 million miles away.   Intimate,
it composes me.   No distant trumpet of Angels.
It burns my skin & enters through my mouth.   A seed

within the apple.   No separation, save convenience.
Judging by its fruits, I taste of it.   Calling to mind, you—
this *extra*sensory persuasion.   We rub in thought
& matter confirms our sweat & friction.   The Uni-

verse remains—as explanation atrophies & the comforts
we forge encode themselves on the headlines of
our front pages.   These roots in—our eyes—nourish
in the earth of Angels to cultivate this double vision . . .

Yes the orb is only 1 focus.   & 100 years, no distance—
Says Emily: "Crowned—Crowing—on my Father's breast—"

Bill Vartnaw was born 35 years ago at General Hospital, Petaluma, California
& continues to be born at all hours of the day. Enjoyed four years at UC Davis
where he read Leibniz & missed hills & redwood trees. Moved to S. F. in 1973,
looked for a community of poets & keeps finding it. Member of the Order of
the Blue Scarf. Previous publication: *If You Should Die a Fool, You Will Be No Less
Wiser for It* (Mini-Taur Series, 1976). This is his first book.